Merle
Thanks so much!
We had a great time in
Phoenix

Eddie Bryan
(Jerry Dixon's
cousin)

Linda Caldwell
(J. Dixon's sister)

Copyright © 2004 Clock Tower Press, LLC

Clock Tower Press, LLC
3622 W. Liberty
Ann Arbor, MI 48103
www.clocktowerpress.com

For corporate or quantity sales please contact our sales department 1-800-956-8999

Printed and bound in the United States.

10 9 8 7 6 5 4 3 2 1

Library of Congress Cataloging-in-Publication Data on file.
ISBN: 1-932202-16-1

Contents

Introduction

I grew up in Des Moines, Iowa and attended an art school in Chicago after graduating from Cornell College in Mount Vernon, Iowa. Twenty-one years ago, I started drawing editorial cartoons for a handful of weekly business newspapers published by Crain Communications in Chicago. About 8 years ago, I received a call from the editors of *Golfweek* asking if I'd be interested in providing a weekly editorial cartoon for their publication. It was a baptism by fire into the world of professional golf.

I have been privileged to work with an unusually creative bunch of editors at *Golfweek*. Over the years, they have taught me that there is no such thing as a "sand trap" and that "golf" is a noun. I have also had the good fortune to be an active observer as Tiger Woods played his way through his final amateur days and entered the ranks of the PGA.

Professional golf is filled with talented players who are plagued by the same challenges as the casual weekend golfer (getting the ball in the cup). Perhaps that is why the professional game appeals to us hackers. Philosophers like to say that the journey is more important than the ending. This is certainly true in golf. The ups and down of the game are what make it interesting for me as an editorial cartoonist and chronicler of the weekly contests.

Included in *Drawn to Golf* are my observations, critiques, and acknowledgments of the world of professional golf. I have tried to relate the story of this world within the contents of this collection. Enjoy!

~ *Roger Schillerstrom*

Georgia on My Mind

The Masters Tournament is the cream of the majors and the official start of all things 'golf' each season. To play the course at Augusta National is a humbling experience for even the best on the PGA Tour. The Masters Committee is an adjunct to the very private and extremely elite Augusta National Golf Club. As such, the tournament found itself at the center of protests in 2003 by some activist women's groups who object to the club's de facto exclusion of women. Whether it's rain, wind, sun, or protests...spring always comes and, with it, the playing of The Masters.

April 15, 1995

January 4, 1997

Greg Norman entered the final round of 1996 six strokes up and ended five strokes down. Faldo went on to win.

April 20, 1996

1996 WAS FILLED WITH A LOT OF FIRSTS...

- HONDA CLASSIC . . . . TIM HERRON
- BAY HILL INVITATIONAL . . . . . PAUL GOYDOS
- FREEPORT/McDERMOTT
    CLASSIC . . . . SCOTT McCARRON
- BELLSOUTH CLASSIC . . . . . P. STANKOWSKI
- KEMPER OPEN . . . . STEVE STRICKER
- DEPOSIT GUARANTY
    GOLF CLASSIC . . . . WILLIE WOOD
- BUICK OPEN . . . . JUSTIN LEONARD
- SPRINT INTERNATIONAL . . . CLARENCE ROSE
- GREATER VANCOUVER
    OPEN . . . . GUY BOROS
- BELL CANADIAN OPEN . . . . . DUDLEY HART
- BUICK CHALLENGE . . . . . MICHAEL BRADLEY
- LAS VEGAS INVITATIONAL . . . TIGER WOODS
- LA CANTERA TEXAS OPEN . . . . DAVID OGRIN

AND ONE GLARING SECOND....

MASTERS

SCHILLERSTROM
GOLFWEEK©96

December 21, 1996

"HEY, KUCHAR...TURN OFF THE SMILE, DUDE! WE'RE TRYING TO GET SOME SLEEP!!"

Mark O'Meara won the 1998 Masters tournament and U.S. Amateur Champion Matt Kuchar won the crown with his unabashed enthusiasm.

April 18, 1998

After Tiger Woods' mastery of Augusta National, the club began a series of steps to make the course more challenging.

April 3, 1999

The Masters' committee has toyed with the idea of having the players use a 'Masters Ball'.

March 30, 2002

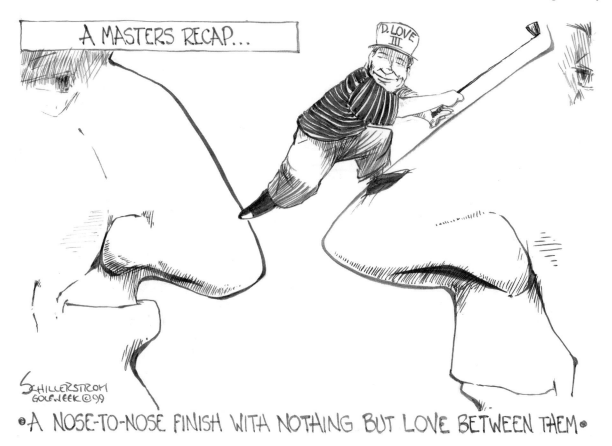

A NOSE-TO-NOSE FINISH WITH NOTHING BUT LOVE BETWEEN THEM

Jose Maria Olazabel won a second Masters. He went into the final round one stroke ahead of Greg Norman and two strokes ahead of Davis Love, III. He ended the day two strokes better than Davis Love, III and three better than Greg Norman.

April 17, 1999

• MASTERS 2000: EYE OF THE STORM •

The wind blew hard in 2000 and Vijay Singh won by three strokes.

April 15, 2000

Tiger Woods wins a second Masters title in 2001, completing an unofficial Grand Slam with four consecutive major victories.

April 14, 2001

The Masters Committee re-wrote its eligibility rules, effective in 2004. Their research came up short when someone realized that the new rules would make Jack Nicklaus ineligible to play the tournament.

May 11, 2002

Tiger Woods won a third Masters title in 2002, posting 12 under par during the tournament's four days of play. 2003 was a different story...

April 19, 2003

Augusta National and the Masters Committee announce a 'reconsideration' of its proposed eligibility rules.

April 5, 2003

The National Council of Women's Organizations demanded that Augusta National put a woman on the membership rolls at the club. Hootie Johnson responded.

July 20, 2002

October 19, 2002

With the threat of advertiser boycotts orchestrated by the protesting women's groups, the Masters Committee decides to go commercial-free in 2003.

April 8, 2003

Mike Weir became the first Canadian to win a major...left-handed, too.

May 10, 2003

No Respect, I Tell Ya...

Caddies are the workhorses of the game. They are responsible for hauling the equipment, knowing yardage and conditions on each green. They suggest club choice and provide support and encouragement to their players. They are also put-upon and at times made the scapegoat of a poor season. Still, they persevere.

"TSK, TSK. YOU'RE SHOWING TOO MUCH ANKLE, YOUNG MAN!!!"

The PGA Tour maintains a caddy dress code of long pants. During the heat wave in the summer of 1996, the caddies began requesting to wear shorts. The request fell on deaf ears.

August 24, 1996

The following summer, the USGA did allow shorts to be worn at their sponsored events. The PGA tour has since permitted 'authorized' shorts to be worn by caddies.

June 14, 1997

In 1997, the Internal Revenue Service decided they were missing out on some untapped revenues and announced they'd be going after the presumably unrecorded tips that caddies on all the courses in the country earn.

1997

26

"CONGRATULATIONS! WE HAD A CHANGE OF HEART...<u>THIS</u> YEAR!"

By Thanksgiving, the I.R.S. had a change of heart.

1997

The PGA Tour had an idea in 2001 to create 'ShotLink', a statistical system that tracks the players shot-by-shot. The idea relies on the players' caddies voluntarily supplying the club selection...without compensation. The caddies continue to balk.

February 17, 2001

March 3, 2001

May 15, 1999

November 20, 1999

For all that they do, caddies are still as expendable at the end of the season as baseball coaches are.

September 16, 2000

Tea for Three (Other Majors)

After the Masters Tournament come, in succession, The U.S. Open, The British Open and the PGA Championship. They've been competing much longer than I've been drawing cartoons about them, so I simply offer some highlights from recent history.

•THE WINNER, AND STILL U.S. OPEN CHAMP, SHINNECOCK HILLS•

Corey Pavin won his first major and was the only player on the Shinnecock Hills course to play even par over four rounds.

June 24, 1995

The Congressional Country Club course was vintage U.S. Open material. Only three broke par for the tournament and Ernie Els finished on top.

June 21, 1997

The USGA decided to offer Special Exemptions to 6 players at the U.S. Open in 2000, based not on meeting the tournament criteria but on nostalgia. The action effectively denied entry to 6 players who could have entered the tournament.

June 10, 2000

Tiger captured his third career major, winning at the Pebble Beach Golf Links with a record 15-stroke win. The victory was all the more remarkable because of the blustery conditions during the tournament.

June 24, 2000

•TIGER WINS THE TROPHY; BETH PAGE WINS THE OPEN•

Tiger Woods beat the U.S. Open field for a second time in 2002, playing on the Bethpage Black public course in Farmingdale, New York. He won this time by 3 strokes, beating out Phil Mickelson.

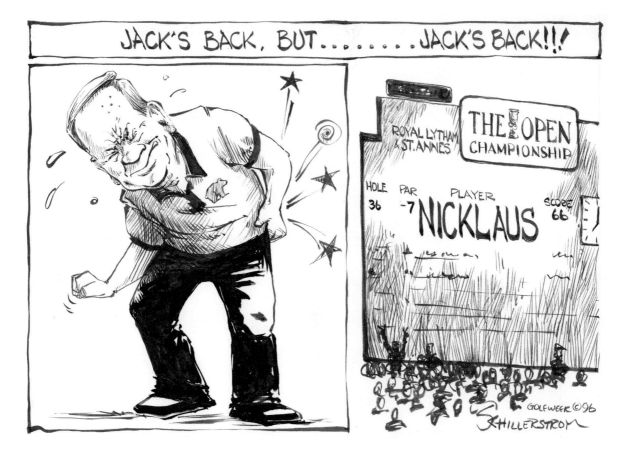

Tom Lehman may have won the 1996 British open but the thrill of the weekend was watching Jack Nicklaus play the second round. Despite suffering severe back pains going into the weekend.

July 27, 1996

Course conditions at the Royal and Ancient Golf Club of St. Andrews were typically challenging in 1998. Mark O'Meara won (after a 4 hole playoff with Brian Watts) with steady and consistent play.

July 25, 1998

Mark O'Meara won both the Masters and the British open in 1998, making him a very popular fellow.

November 21, 1998

Jean Van de Velde approached the 18th hole of the 1999 British Open with a three-stroke lead. His approach shot found water and he squandered his lead as he tried and tried, and tried again to hit out of the hazard. He lost a four-hole playoff to Paul Lawrie.

July 24th, 1999

"WELCOME TO THIS YEAR'S COVERAGE OF THE 55th U.S. WOMEN'S OPEN GOLF CHAMPIONSHIP."

Poor scheduling in 2000 resulted in the simultaneous playing of the U.S. Women's Open and the British Open.

July 22, 2000

David Duval finished the 2001 British Open Championship with a 10-under 274 total to win by three strokes.

July 28, 2001

•THE HARDEST WORKING MAN IN THE GOLF BUSINESS•

Vijay Singh won the PGA Championship in 1998. It was a deserving win for a hard working golfer known for heading to the driving range even AFTER a full day of tournament golf to practice on his swing.

August 22, 1998

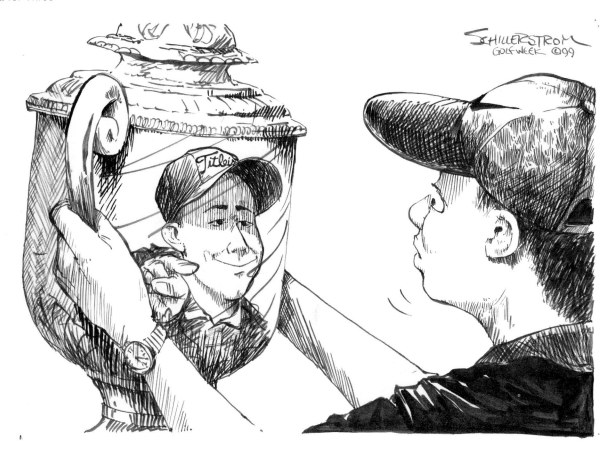

Tiger Woods garnered the PGA Championship trophy in 1999. Sergio Garcia proved a talent to be reckoned with, however. In his rookie season in the PGA tour, he finished just one stroke behind Woods.

August 21, 1999

· LOUISVILLE SLUGGERS ·

Although Tiger Woods won the PGA Championship in 2000, Bob May put up quite a fight.

August 26, 2000

Shaun Micheel was just hoping to make the cut going into the 2003 PGA Championship...and walked away a winner.

August 23, 2003

Tale of a Tiger

Tiger Woods' entrance onto the national stage was highly anticipated. After winning an unprecedented third consecutive national amateur title, the speculation was intense. He chose the Greater Milwaukee Open for his professional debut. Since joining the Tour, Tiger has matured and grown as a competitor. In the process, he has proven himself to be the best player in the world.

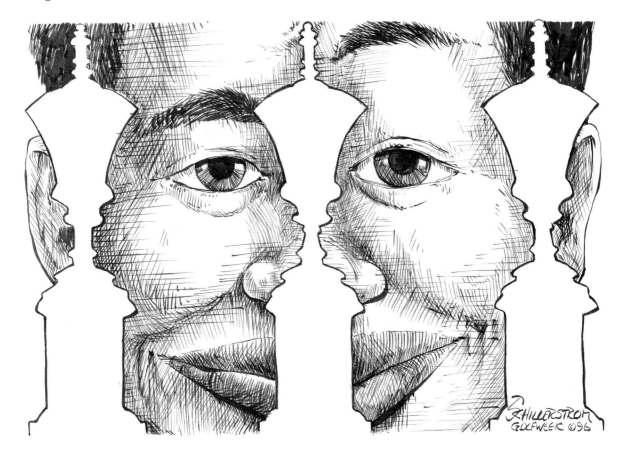

Tiger Woods won an unprecedented third consecutive U.S. Amateur Championship and set the stage for beginning his pro career.

August 31, 1996

The magic still prevails four years later, as Tiger proves to be a tremendous drawing card.

May 6, 2000

July 21, 2001

"IF LOAVES AND FISHES FELL FROM THE SKY, I WOULDN'T BE SURPRISED!!"

Tiger chose the obscure Milwaukee Open as the venue for his first tournament as a pro. He tied for 60th, winning a whopping $2,544 and also registering his first ace as a pro.

Sept. 7, 1996

"NOT EVEN JET LAG CAN DAMPEN THE EXCITEMENT OF BEING HERE. RIGHT, TIGER...?"

Tiger travels to his mother's native Thailand.

February 15, 1997

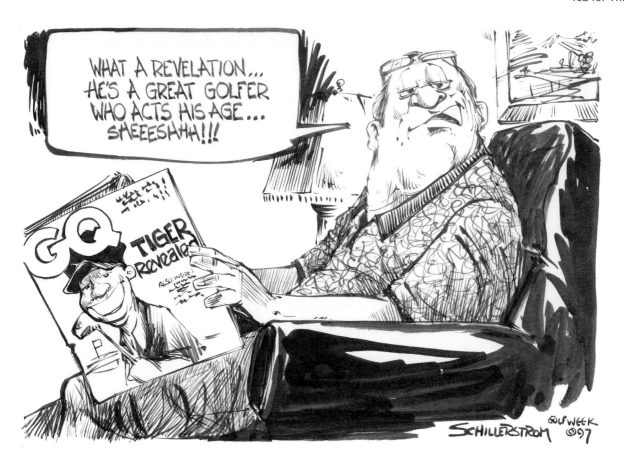

Amid all of the hype and hoopla, GQ runs a profile of Tiger and discovers something we suspected all along....

April 5, 1997

Speculation was rampant. Was Tiger African-American, Asian-American, Native-American.... And what did it really matter?

May 3, 1997

ADDITIONAL REMOVEABLE IMPEDIMENTS TO AFFORD GREATER SUCCESS FOR TIGER ....

ROCKS STICKS DAVID DUVAL

During a Phoenix tournament, Tiger's ball landed inconveniently behind a boulder. Several gallery members helped him roll it out of the way.

February 13, 1999

Tiger may not be the only competitor on the Tour prone to temper tantrums... but he is the most noticed.

July 1, 2000

The challenge from week to week is who will provide competition to play against Tiger's game?

June 3, 2000

Tiger's dominance on Tour obscures so many in the field, that perhaps they should consider invoking a seldom-used rule....

June 29, 2002

Tiger signs an endorsement contract with Nike worth an estimated $100 million over five years.

September 23, 2000

In 2002, talk of a true 'Grand Slam' began anew as Tiger started the year with wins at both The Masters, and the U.S. Open. Unfortunately, he finished second at the PGA Championship.

August 3, 2002

"I'M WORRIED...TIGER HASN'T NABBED A BIRD IN WEEKS!!!"

The talk is either about Tiger winning or why he is not winning....

March 17, 2001

Of course, if only other players could have the kind of 'slump' that Tiger experiences!

July 12, 2003

Tiger underwent microscopic knee surgery and was sidelined at the beginning of 2003.

January 17, 2003

Ernie Els started 2003 with two consecutive wins at the Mercedes Championship and the Sony Open... but then Tiger rejoined the Tour, promptly winning the Buick Invitational.

February 22, 2003

67

Tiger finished the 2003 Tour season with 5 victories out of 17 starts adding up to 39 career victories since turning pro in 1996.

October 11, 2003

Hands Across the Water

The Ryder Cup matches began in 1927 in Worchester, Massachusetts. The two teams (the U.S. and Great Britain/Ireland) have played in alternating years for 34 times. The U.S. leads the overall series 24-8-2, but Europe has earned the gold trophy six of the last nine meetings.

The long history of competition places an anticipation and pressure on its participants. The recent history of wins and losses reflects the skill and seriousness that now accompanies each meeting across the water.

Captain of the 1995 U.S. Ryder Cup team was Lanny Watkins.

August 12, 1995

"SORRY, MR. GALLACHER, BUT WE DON'T DO 'VICTORY ROLLS' ON THE CONCORDE!"

The 1995 Ryder Cup was played in Rochester, New York and won by Europe, 14 1/2 to 13 1/2.

September 30, 1995

Woe be to the captain of a losing Ryder Cup team. The hat is passed to Tom Kite, captain of the 1997 U.S. Ryder Cup team.

November 25, 1995

Dolly the sheep proved cloning is possible, and suddenly putting together a winning U.S. team also seemed possible.

March 15, 1997

Led by Tiger Woods, the 1997 U.S. team that headed to Valderrama, Spain seemed unstoppable on paper.

September 13, 1997

Europe: 14 1/2. U.S.: 13 1/2.

October 4, 1997

The U.S. pulled out a victory in 1999. The winning putt was made by Justin Leonard. The infamously exuberant U.S. victory celebration on the 17th green was roundly criticized by Europe. U.S. 14 1/2, Europe 13 1/2.

October 2, 1999

"...AND THE CAPTAIN'S PICKS FOR EUROPE ARE...."

Europe's system of choosing its Ryder Cup team leaves little choice for its captains.

September 8, 2001

A European team of relative unknowns was expertly captained by Sam Torrance and decisively beat the U.S. 15 1/2-12 1/2.

October 5, 2002

There's Gold in Them Thar Hills

One hundred and twenty-five PGA Tour players retain their Tour cards each year. Those who do not earn enough tournament money to be in the top group must either quit the Tour, play in one of the many developmental tours and rejoin the Tour after finishing in the top tier of those developmental tours, or join other Tour hopefuls in Qualification School at the end of the year. Q School is a grueling, tension-filled six days of make-or-break golf. The winners get the prized Tour Card, and a chance to earn the big bucks on the PGA Tour.

At the other end of the earnings rainbow is the Champions Tour. The Champions Tour began in 1980 as the Senior Tour. It was formed as a nostalgia tour for the popular players over 50 who were no longer competitive on the PGA Tour. It's nice work if you can get it...

October 26, 1996

December 2, 1995

December 7, 1996

October 25, 1996

December 13, 1997

November 28, 1996

December 9, 2000

Hale Irwin celebrated his 50th birthday in the Summer of 1995. The competitive nature of the Senior Tour was about to change.

October 14, 1995

For those who qualify for the Senior Tour, the winnings are easy money.

March 9, 1996

October 18, 1997

By February, there seemed to be a certain pattern to Senior Tour winners...either Irwin or Morgan.

February 14, 1998

Hale Irwin wins an amazing three in a row Seniors Championships.

April 25, 1998

In the year 2000, Tom Watson and Tom Kite joined Allan Doyle on the Senior Tour.

February 12, 2000

The U.S. Senior Open took a chance and played at a smaller market venue. The gamble paid off.

July 17, 1999

The Senior Tour realized that it had gotten away from the fan-friendly interactions that typified the tour in its earlier years.

November 3, 2001

There's Gold in Them Thar Hills!

PGA Tour Commissioner Tim Finchem announces a concerted effort to expand the Senior Tour's base of fan support.

December 1, 2001

The Senior Tour changes its name.

November 16/23, 2002

Lady Players Golfing with Annika

The LPGA always seems to be the tour in search of an identity. The women are skilled professionals who offer exciting competition at each tournament. Even so, prize money pales next to the men's tour and media exposure is slim by comparison.

Annika Sorenstam is a powerhouse player who may succeed in lifting the LPGA to the level of attention it deserves. It's a prospect worth watching for.

June 15, 1999

In an attempt to garner some positive press, the LPGA signs model Kathy Ireland as sponsor.

March 11, 2000

CBS Sports announcer Ben Wright's analysis of the LPGA's image problems reflected more on his image than on the LPGA's image.

June 3, 1995

Muffin Spencer-Devlin chose to discuss her sexuality in a national sports publication. The sky did not fall...and the world kept spinning.

March 23, 1996

Laura Davies' alarm didn't ring the final day of the 1996 Tour Championship. She went on to finish in a tie for fifth.

November 30, 1996

Juli Inkster makes it a grand slam in 1999.

July 3, 1999

Later that same year, Juli Inkster is inducted into the LPGA Hall of Fame. The announcement coincided with the playing of the Ryder Cup and an overly celebratory U.S. team.

October 2, 1999

In 2002, Juli Inkster won her second U.S. Women's Open Championship, defeating Annika Sorenstam by two strokes.

July 13, 2002

In her 1996 rookie year, Karrie Webb became the first woman to win more than $1 million in a season. She completed a Career Grand Slam after winning the McDonald's LPGA championship.

June 30, 2001

The tradition at the Nabisco Championship is for the winner to dive into Champions Lake at the 18th hole. After her third win of 2001, Sorenstam was flying, not diving.

March 31, 2001

Sorenstam was ranked #1 in the LPGA by the Summer of 2001, but Karrie Webb was not giving up without a fight.

June 9, 2001

November 17, 2001

Annika Sorenstam joined an elite group of players, shooting a second round 59 en route to winning the Standard Register Ping tournament.

March 24, 2001

Early in 2003, Annika Sorenstam expressed an interest in PGA tour competition. She had several takers...

February 1, 2003

Sorenstam entered the Bank of America Colonial golf tournament. Kenny Perry won, Sorenstam failed to make the cut. You wouldn't have guessed it by the press coverage.

May 31, 2003

Rules, Rules, Rules

It's a hard job serving as policeman to an evolving industry. Advances in technology have created better equipment and advances in physical training have created better players. Still, the integrity of the game must be preserved and the burden falls upon the USGA to do so.

"WHY? BASICALLY, WE'RE BORED AND CAN'T THINK OF ANYTHING ELSE TO DO!"

In 1997, the USGA thought that shaft length might be giving an unfair advantage to players.

February 8, 1997

...MORE SUGGESTIONS TO ASSIST THE USGA IN PRESERVING GOLF'S INTEGRITY AND TRADITIONS:

COURSE TRANSPORTATION

GOLF BALLS

COURSE ATTIRE

June 6, 1998

In 1998, the USGA set its sights on club head size and their spring-like effect. In particular, they focused on the equipment being introduced by the Callaway Company.

October 10, 1998

• USGA EXECUTIVE COMMITTEE MEETING, FALL 1998 •

It's hard to imagine a more dry subject matter that discussion of spring-like effect, club head weight and club shaft lengths. Yawn.

November 17, 1998

The British rules-making body sets the standards for areas outside the United States. The USGA sets rules and standards inside the United States. Oftentimes, the R&A uses a less-labored, draconian process to make its decisions which results in beating the USGA to the punch.

September 30, 2000

The job can be overwhelming at times....

October 7, 2000

IDENTIFYING THE UNFAIR ADVANTAGE.

It was suggested that the culprit of the longer hitting game is the ball.

May 12, 2001

Ride or Wrong?

As professional golf entered 1998, it was being forced to deal with an issue of fairness in competition: if a player is talented enough to play on tour but is physically handicapped, should that player be permitted to participate in tournament play?

Casey Martin was born with a rare circulatory disorder that makes his right leg extremely weak. Kippel-Treaunay-Weber syndrome inflicted great pain when walking and, in fact, made walking extremely risky for Martin.

Martin rode in a golf cart in competition. He won the Nike Lakeland Classic on the Nationwide Tour in 1998 and earned his 2000 PGA Tour card the following year. The PGA Tour would argue that a player must play "under his own Power" and that riding in a cart in competition violated that rule. Martin mounted a legal challenge under the Americans with Disabilities Act.

December 20/27, 1997

January 17, 1998

Casey Martin won the first round. The PGA Tour appealed.

February 21, 1998

While on appeal, the PGA Tour allows Martin to ride in competition.

November 6, 1999

March 18, 2000

Despite losing its lower court appeal, the PGA Tour decides to carry the issue all of the way to the Supreme Court.

June 17, 2000

The U.S. Supreme Court rules in the PGA Tour v. Martin that use of a cart by a disabled player does NOT fundamentally change the nature of tournament golf.

June 22, 2001

'Nuff Said

As I sorted through the editorial work I've done over the past eight years, I ran across some favorites that were not numerous enough to include in a stand-alone chapter. Included in this mix are several cartoons focused on the endorsement season, the quest for better equipment, 'in remembrance' pieces, and a few others. Enjoy.

"DRAT! A WHOLE NEW SEASON AND ALL I HAVE TO WEAR ARE LAST YEAR'S ENDORSEMENTS!"

January 18, 1997

"HI, DORIS...IF ANYONE WANTS ME, JUST TELL THEM I'M OUT CLIENT-PROSPECTING!"

2000

October 19, 1996

THE NEXT BIG STEP IN CUSTOMIZED GOLF BALLS.....

EUREKA!
I'VE DONE IT!!!

A BALL FOR BLONDE,
LEFT-HANDERS,
PLAYING TITANIUM CLUBS
AT AUGUSTA NATIONAL
DURING THE MONTH OF
APRIL IN A LEAP YEAR!!!

SCHILLERSTROM
GOLFWEEK ©98

March 14, 1998

1998

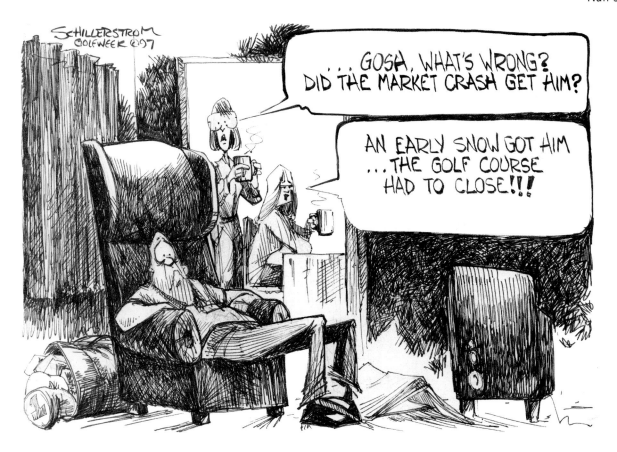

1997

1999

"SALT WATER SEEPING INTO FLORIDA'S FRESH WATERS? DON'T BE RIDICULOUS!!!"

2001

"GOD'S RUNNING LATE TODAY...HE'S GETTING FITTED FOR SOME NEW IRONS...."

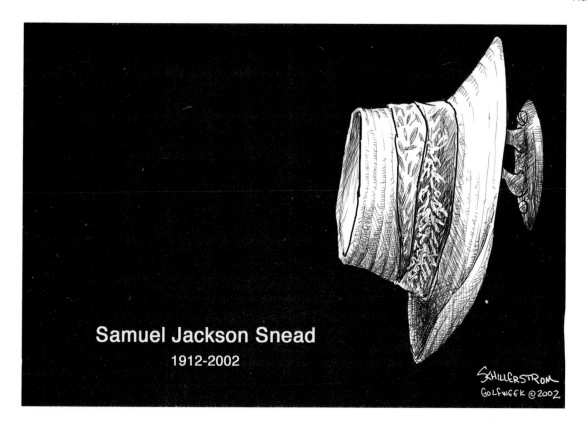

Samuel Jackson Snead

1912-2002

Golf Books as Timeless as the Game.

The **Clock Tower Press** library of over 50 golf titles includes spectacular photographic books on golf course architecture and design, golf instruction, fiction, history and humor. Our books cover classic courses such as St. Andrews, Pebble Beach and Augusta National.

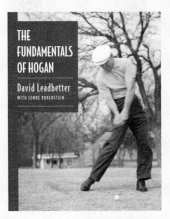

The Fundamentals of Hogan

By David Leadbetter
Retail Price: $14.95

Five Lessons, Ben Hogan's 1957 book on the golf swing, is still considered to be one of the finest instructional books ever written. The photographs that were used in the preparation of Hogan's book were recently rediscovered. These famous photos are now revealed in *The Fundamentals of Hogan*, a book by David Leadbetter. Leadbetter uses these remarkable images of the master at work to demonstrate the basic techniques of golf to a new generation.

Augusta National & The Masters: A Photographer's Scrapbook

By Frank Christian with Cal Brown
Retail Price: $19.95

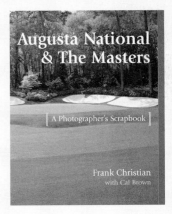

Few places are as beautiful as the Augusta National Golf Club, and few tournaments are as prestigious as The Masters. This book is a special history of these two famous names in golf. This classic must-have golf volume has been completely updated with current Masters history. Available for the first time in softcover, this full-color title captures the Masters like no other book.

The Life of O'Reilly:
The Amusing Adventures of a Professional Irish Caddie

By John O'Reilly & Ivan Morris
Retail Price: $10.95

Over the course of 50 years John O'Reilly became one of European golf's most famous—some would say "infamous"—caddies. *The Life of O'Reilly* is a chronicle of John's career, and to read it is to feel like you are in the clubhouse, having a pint, and hearing the stories of a lifetime. *The Life of O'Reilly*, a rollicking ride around the world of professional golf, there is never a dull page.

Golf Nuts: You've Got To Be Committed

By Ron Garland with Brian Hewitt
Foreword and chapter on "Golf Nut #23" Michael Jordan - featuring his golf stories you won't believe!
Retail Price: $18.95

An in-depth recounting of the founding of the Golf Nuts Society and an intimate look into the mind of the man (Garland) who started "the most unique golf association in the world." All golfers are at least a little nuts about the game, and will relate to the antics of the Society members.

Caddywhack! A Kid's-Eye View of Golf

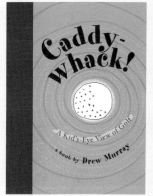

by Drew Murray
Retail Price: $14.95

Discover that a golf course is not just for golf, that there is a community of golf, that there are hazards to avoid and what are the most important things in golf. As a parent, you will learn about how to let kids enjoy a sport for what it is, from their perspective—a kid's-eye view. And then just get out of the way.

The Wit & Wisdom of Bobby Jones

by Sidney L. Matthew
Retail Price: $14.95

Sportsmen continue to marvel that Bobby Jones's legacy remains unparalleled in golf history. One of the reasons why is because Jones was more than the consummate champion golfer. This collection of quotes captures his spirit.

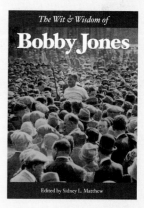

CLOCK TOWER PRESS

Corporate and volume sales are available for all titles.
Please call 1-800-956-8999.
Clock Tower Press, 3622 W. Liberty, Ann Arbor, MI 48103
www.clocktowerpress.com • www.huronriverpress.com.